Günter Freun… …Cookbook

Günter Freund

Günter Freund's Swabian Cookbook

66 Selected Recipes
for Connoisseurs
of the Swabian Art of Cooking

Including 6 Cartoons by Heinz Schindele
and 4 Color Illustrations

2nd edition

Hugo Matthaes
Druckerei und Verlag
GmbH & Co. KG
Stuttgart

ISBN 3-87516-097-5

Recipe consultation: Gardy Freund
Title photo: Bildniskunst Dittmar, Stuttgart
English translation by
Christa Veil

Printed in Germany – Imprimé en Allemagne

Total production:
Hugo Matthaes Druckerei und Verlag
GmbH & Co. KG, Stuttgart

Foreword

Those who are familiar with the charming conversationalist of many entertainment programs of the Süddeutscher Rundfunk (Radio Station of Southern Germany) know, that he is to be included on the list of gourmets; also, that he is a superior hobby-cook indeed. During many of his radio programs, in which also famous German chef de cuisines contributed their parts, he provided an answer, with his collection of national and international recipes, to listening housewives' old yet ever-new question "What shall we have for dinner?"

The fact that he published a Swabian cookbook deserves not only praise. It is actually a matter of honor for a Swabian!

The Swabian cuisine is often unjustly accused of being solid and heavy (as in lots of calories and fattening). This cuisine is mainly tasty and versatile, which Günter Freund will prove with a few tricks and knacks.

Due to trips around the world and many international restaurants in our country, our cuisine has been strongly influenced on an international basis. We cook and dine French, Italian, Greek, Chinese, and even Indian. This is not to be discredit-

ed. It only proves how internationally aware we Swabians really are.
However, as soon as we simply, once again, focus our attention on our fellow countrymen with a sense of pride, our culinary trends return – should I say – to more basic meals, to home cooking, as we enjoyed and cherished in our grandparents' homes.
In any case, it pleases me that our Swabian cuisine should once again be regarded more highly. Our cuisine can most definitely be included on the palette of specialities and is today no longer just a matter of filling the stomach. Firstly, our taste buds are given the pleasure.
Eating is one of life's pleasures. Many a time we remember a certain occasion so well only because we know exactly what delicious dish had been served. Hopefully, Günter Freund's Swabian Cookbook will cause many a stranger to remember a good Swabian meal, our beautiful "Schwabenland" and the fact that we Swabians – young and old alike – and all those who have found a homeland here, give our Swabian cuisine the honor it deserves.
May I add that regardless of festive meals served here and there, my husband and children have remained "fans" of the Swabian cuisine. This booklet will not only become a part of my cookbook

collection, I will take it to hand, flip the pages, dwell on memories – and most importantly of all, serve those dishes that have kept the Swabian tradition alive.

May many housewives and "cooking men" join me in this effort; this I personally wish Günter Freund and his Swabian Cookbook.

Ursula Späth

(Patroness of the Multiple Sclerosis Foundation AMSEL and wife of Lothar Späth, former Minister-President of the State of Baden-Württemberg, Federal Republic of Germany).

I About Myself, He About Himself

Actually, one would not want to grant him the permission to write a Swabian cookbook. He was not even born under the Swabian sun, but rather up north, near the river Main.

"However," responds a fully-grown Swabian, "he went to school here, in Untertürkheim and Bad Cannstatt. For that reason one cannot characterize him as being at best an adopted Swabian, he is definitely one of us!" Having been to such a great extent generously accepted, I admit: I enjoy being a real Swabian for several reasons. One reason being the Swabian cuisine, which, when compared to the accustomed home cooking of the State of Hessen of already forgotten childhood memories – only remembering the fact that this young lad most definitely did not enjoy eating spinach – is after all not too different.

The first career goal was to become a teacher ("because they have so much vacation time off"), however, soon thereafter, a journalist I wanted to become. The first contact made with printer's ink was at a publishing house. Someone felt that I had a pleasant voice. Therefore, intensive speech training from an actor in Stuttgart. The first assignment at a radio television station – completely miscasted – the part of a doctor consulting two women with flat feet and vericose veins. Right from the beginning announcer of “top hits” and for 23 years thereafter. Among the many subsequent programs the “Kochkunstklause” (cooking talent club) with gourmet chefs at the studio, who answered listeners’ (mostly female) questions relating to kitchen secrets. Today, patient conversational partner during the telephone program “Sie wünschen, wir spielen” (which song can we play for you) and announcer for the traditional “Hitparade” (hit countdown). 10 years columnist for a daily newspaper and an informational organization in Stuttgart. On stages and podiums conferences and moderations for fashion shows, folklore evenings, representative presentations (e. g. the World Championship of Hairdressers) and exhibitions for the Hotel and Motel Association (Intergastra). The Chaîne des Rôtisseurs, of which I enjoy being a member, honored me with the position of Chargé de Presse (press representative). Personal details: happily married to Gardy (graceful, blond, clever and the best cook I know). She is also spiritus rector when it comes to creating new and preserving old cooking recipes.

More personal details: trips to all corners of the world, thereafter concerts, mixing cocktails, stylish dining in the fortunately numerous high-class restaurants here in Baden-Württemberg. Inviting friends to our apartment on the 19th floor.

Doesn't the sign of Gemini seem somewhat noticeable?

The "Bund der Kriegsblinden Deutschlands" (Association of the War-Blind of the Federal Republic of Germany) presented me with the Gold Honorary Medal, of which I am very proud. I have moderated this association's publication for many years and read literature via cassette recordings (to date 12 dozen books) at the Library for the Blind.

The first publishing of "50 Meisterköche Baden-Württembergs" (50 superior chefs of Baden-Württemberg, Idee Publishing House) was already out-of-print after 7 months, which although being positive, was however, also a shame.

My personal wish to the reader: may this collection of recipes provide you with the enthusiasm to "serve a new dish" ... even if the recipe is an old one.

Ihr Günter Freund

Günter Freund

Table of Contents

Soups and Stews

Gaisburger Marsch
Potato and Noodle Stew

An old section of the city of Stuttgart (the eastern part) gave this typical Swabian stew its name; it is also known as "Kartoffelschnitz und Spatzen."

First, prepare "Spätzle," the Swabian "national noodle." You will need 1¾ cups flour, 2 eggs, ~~½ cup~~ and ~~2 tablespoons lukewarm water~~, 1 teaspoon salt. Combine ingredients and beat well until air blisters form and until the dough ceases to cling to the spoon during testing, by holding spoon up in the air. Dip a wooden cutting board in cold water, spread some noodle dough on board and scrape (with a knife or rubber scraper) thin strips into rapidly boiling salted water. As soon as the "Spätzle" rise to the surface, remove with slotted spoon, rinse shortly in hot water and place in colander to drain. Instead of scraping ("schaben") by hand, you may press dough through a "Spätzlesschwob," (a Special Swabian noodle-press), which can be purchased in a household goods store.

Gaisburger Marsch is based on a strong meat stock. In approx. 5 cups stock cook 18 ounces peeled and quartered potatoes until tender, but not too soft. Add finely chopped beef, from which the stock was prepared, and the "Spätzles." Season again, adding additional stock if desired. Add a dash nutmeg and sprinkle minced chives over top.

A rich ("aushausig") version calls for cooking in meat stock and in addition topping with sautéed onion.

Eggs, then add
flour - little by little

Schwäbische Hochzeitssuppe
Swabian Wedding Soup

As the name already indicates, this recipe is a very special and naturally extravagant dinner entrée, consisting of "Maultaschen" (ravioli-like noodle squares, filled with meat-mixture), "Flädle" (thin pancake strips made from salted batter) and "Markklößchen" (bone-marrow-dumplings) served in a soup stock. All ingredients are equally important. The Swabian culture would never permit the strong beef stock to be omitted. Into the beef stock we cut thin strips of fried pancakes/crêpes (recipe on page 114).

The bone-marrow dumplings are prepared from the following: 3½ tablespoons marrow, 3 tablespoons milk, 2 tablespoons butter, 2 eggs, 1 teaspoon minced parsley, bread crumbs and a dash of salt. Soak bone marrow in water for ½ hour, then cook in the milk until lightly transparent. Then press through sieve. Add slightly heated butter to marrow-mixture and beat with fork or whisk until creamy. Add eggs, parsley and bread crumbs and mix lightly until mixture can be shaped. Moisten hands and mold tiny dumplings (thimble-sized). Drop into boiling beef stock and simmer for 5 minutes.

Now the dumplings are done. Remove dumplings with slotted spoon and set aside.

Prepare "Maultaschen" according to the famous recipe (page 118), however, smaller, approximately 1¼ by 1¼ inches, slightly larger than ravioli squares.

Pour one large ladle full beef stock into a heated soup dish, then add a heaping tablespoonful pancake strips, followed by 5 bone-marrow dumplings and the same number of "Maultaschen," being careful not to pile into dish, but arrange in a manner appealing to the eye, thus in three sections. Sprinkle minced chives and a dash freshly ground nutmeg over top.

This soup will not only impress wedding guests, it can ideally be served on any festive occasion.

**Greifet Sie nur zu.
Was auf em Tisch steht,
isch scho verschmerzt**

*(Just help yourself.
What's on the table has already
been calculated in costwise)*

Schwäbische Brotsuppe

Swabian Bread Soup

Pour enough hot water, until just covered, over 1 small loaf dry (day-old) bread and one “Laugenbrezel” (pretzel-roll). You may substitute with one level cup pretzel sticks, broken into small pieces. The dark pretzel-crust of this special Swabian roll provides the desired flavor. Let soak. In the meantime sauté in a large pot ½ cup oil, 1 cup minced onion, ½ cup carrots and 1 tablespoon finely chopped celery root (also called celeriac or celerirave) until onion is light-yellow in color. Add 2 whole cloves garlic and the soaked bread (squeeze out liquid and tear into small pieces). Add enough of water mixture to cover.

Cook (covered) for 1 hour, stirring occasionally, then press through sieve. Return to pot and simmer at low heat. Season to taste with coarse black pepper, a bouillon cube and dry white wine (Riesling). If necessary, add more water.

If this soup is to be served alone as a main dish, 2 frankfurters (1 "Pärle Saiten") per person should be added and heated in soup. This soup tastes good and will "fill you up" until the next meal (das schmeckt gut und "hebt" bis zum "Veschper").

Wenn m'r a guete Supp' hat,
hat m'r halbe gessa

(A hearty soup is half a meal!)

Biersuppe
Beer Soup

Back in the good old days beer bottle crates could not be found stacked in German households, empty ones to be exchanged for ones with filled bottles. One purchased beer from the neighborhood tavern and carried it home in a lidless pitcher. The following soup recipe dates back to those very same days, which somehow have been forgotten. Going along with the nostalgic trend, which does not exclude meals, hot beer soup could very well once again be sampled.

For 4 persons we require 3 bottles beer (7½ cups). Cook in large pot 2 cups beer and 7 tablespoons sugar while stirring constantly. As soon as the sugar is completely dissolved, add the remaining beer. Bring to a boil once more and remove pot from heat.

Beat 4 egg yolks with a whisk in a large bowl, then add ½ cup + 2 tablespoons sour cream, a teaspoon at a time, beating constantly. Now add 1/2 cup of the hot beer stock to the egg yolk-sour cream mixture and beat thoroughly. Then pour back into the hot beer stock and stir well. Simmer at low heat (do not boil) and season with 1/2 teaspoon salt, 1/2 teaspoon ground cinnamon and freshly ground black pepper. Serve this hot soup by pouring over "golden cubes" ("Goldwürfel") bread croûtons (sautéed to a crisp in butter) in heated soup mugs or dishes.

This dish would most certainly be something unusual for your next dinner party (Das wär doch mal was Apartes für die nächste Einladung).

Biersuppe

Leberspätzle in Fleischbrühe

Liver "Spätzle" or Noodles in Meat Stock

Prepare a stiff "Spätzle" (noodle) dough by combining 1¾ cups flour, 2 eggs, 1 level teaspoon salt and ½ cup and 2 tablespoons warm water in a large bowl and beat until air blisters form.

Season 3½ ounces minced beef liver with ground pepper, nutmeg and grated lemon rind. Combine with noodle dough and beat thoroughly.

Press into boiling beef stock through a "Spätzlesschwob" (special Swabian noodle-press) or large-holed colander.

Cook 5 minutes until done. May be served "geschmälzt" (sautéed in butter and minced onion) and minced chives sprinkled over top.

These "Leberspätzle" may be served as an entrée or as a main course.

Brätstrudel-Suppe
"Brätstrudel" Soup

This entrée represents far more than a usual soup dish; is ideal when followed by a light main dinner course or for example a sweet dish or leftovers.
"Brätstrudel" soup requires some preparation. The base consists of a strong beef stock, prepared the day before using beef brisket, soup bones and soup vegetables. Prepare a thin "Flädle-batter" (thin pancake batter) according to recipe on page 114. It is recommended to peel an onion, cut into halves, skewer rounded side onto fork, dip flat side of onion in fat (butter, oil or margarine) and use to grease skillet. Pour only a small quantity of batter into skillet, so that by skillfully tipping the skillet, the batter will only thinly coat the bottom.
These pancakes prepared in this fashion (1 or 2 per person) are then spread with a mixture of "Wurstbrät" (Swabian sausage dressing), consisting of veal, pork and spi-

ces (you may substitute with well-seasoned pork sausage), 1 minced onion and a dash nutmeg. Roll and place in deep, heated soup dishes. Pour hot beef stock over top and garnish with minced fresh chives.

Des isch ebbes Arg's, was i Wurscht essa muaß, bis meine Kender von de' Zipfel satt werdet

(Hard to believe how many sausages I have to eat for my children to finally have filled their bellies on the sausage ends!)

Saubohneneintopf
"Pig-Bean" Stew

One can provide the main ingredient of this dish with a more sophisticated name such as "dicke Bohnen" (fat beans), "Pferdebohnen" (horse beans) or "Puffbohnen" (European light-brown colored dry beans of the legume family - broad beans).

In any case 2 lbs. + 3 ounces dry beans are required. Cook the beans in lightly salted water for approx. 15 minutes (beans must be completely covered). Drain in colander. Sauté 1/2 cup each minced onion and bacon. Add 2 tablespoons butter and 5 1/2 tablespoons flour until mixture is light-yellow in color. Add enough stock or bouillon broth to cover beans, stirring constantly. Season with a dash of sugar, salt, pepper and 1 tablespoon vinegar. Cook beans in this sauce until tender.

This stew is tasty when smoked spareribs or smoked sausage are added before serving.

For those who enjoy a fattier version, an 18-ounce piece of smoked pork (flank) may be cooked in soup, which can most definitely be served cold the next day with mustard and bread.
This stew is a hearty meal, especially on a cold and rainy November day.

Schwäbische Kartoffelsupp' mit Saitenwürstle

Swabian Potato Soup with Sausages

Peel and dice into small pieces approx. 18 ounces potatoes (approx. 5 potatoes) and 3 carrots. Sauté 1 minced onion, 1 bunch minced parsley and a few celery leaves of a celery root (also called celeriac or celeri-rave) in 3½ tablespoons (lard provides the best taste, however, oil or margarine may be substituted) until soft. Then add diced potatoes and carrots. Sprinkle with 1 tablespoon flour, stirring constantly and continue to cook for 5 minutes. Add sufficient amount of bouillon broth and simmer over low heat, covered, for ½ hour. Press soup through sieve and re-heat. Season if required. Add 2 sausages per person, either whole or cut into bite-sized pieces.

To make soup even more special, add "Kracherle" (bread croûtons, browned in butter) and sprinkle over top of soup.

Gemüseeintopf
Vegetable Stew

To prepare a hearty vegetable stew, years ago, the Swabian housewife purchased a variety of fresh vegetables at the town market and worked hard at cleaning and chopping. Today, modern technology offers us deep-freezing, which relieves us of this tedious chore and we can rely on a package of frozen mixed vegetables to be of a superior enough quality for this stew.

In addition 5 large raw potatoes are required. Peel and dice potatoes into cubes and cook in 10 cups well-seasoned meat stock or bouillon broth for 5 minutes. Add vegetables, 5 crushed peppercorns, 2 mashed cloves garlic and 1 bunch minced parsley and cook until tender.

Add a small can beef in its own juice (remove suet) and chop into bite-sized pieces, and, if necessary, recheck seasoning. Leftovers freeze well.

's gibt nix Besseres als ebbes Guats!

(There's nothing better than something tasty!)

The following pages show color photographs of:

"Buabaspitzle" ("Boys' Penises" or Potato Noodles)

"Krautwickel" (Stuffed Cabbage Rolls)

"Linsen mit Spätzle und Saiten"
(Lentil Stew and Spätzle and Sausages)

"Rindsrouladen" (Beef Roulades or Rolls)

Fish Dishes

Bodenseefelchen
Lake Constance Whitefish

These particular whitefish, tasty fellows, originating from Lake Constance, with their blue backs and firm white flesh, can be prepared in many ways. I would like to introduce you to my favorite recipe: Lake Constance whitefish with white wine, baked in aluminum foil.

Allow 1 whitefish per person. Have it cleaned and the scales removed at the store. At home cut off tail and fins with scissors. Clean inside and outside of fish under running water and blot dry with paper towels. Rub inside and outside with lemon juice. Chop equal amounts of carrots and onion and sauté in casserole in oil, adding salt, pepper (freshly ground) and minced garlic, stirring constantly while adding small amounts of dry white wine (Riesling).

Then rub fish inside and out with salt, pepper and cumin, provided you have some on hand (fish can stand heavy seasoning) and then stuff with carrot-onion mixture. Brush double-strength aluminum foil well with oil (for each fish), place fish on top and fold sides up so that 2 tablespoons white wine can be poured over each fish without any leaking out. Add a quarter tomato slice. Fold sides of foil together at top. Using a fork, pierce a few holes in the top for steam to be able to escape.

Place fish packets in preheated oven (rack positioned in center). Bake at medium temperature for 20–30 minutes.

Serve opened foil packets on plates. Serve with boiled potatoes or various salads, if desired. Trout, often reasonably priced, can be prepared in the same manner.

Forelle im "Mandel-Mantel"

Trout in an Almond Jacket

Have trout cleaned at the store. Cut off tail and fins with scissors. Quickly clean under running water and dry thoroughly with paper towels. Season the inside of fish with lemon juice and salt. Sprinkle with a little milk, flour and pepper. Melt a generous amount of butter in pan. Fry fish on both sides until golden in color (not browned!). Place fish on heated platter and place in warm oven. Toast almonds in remaining butter and sprinkle on top of fish. Serve with boiled potatoes (sprinkled with chopped parsley) and lemon wedges. Prepared in this manner even the skin is tasty. Since fish insist on swimming, a bottle of dry white wine (Riesling) served alongside would do just fine.

Schwäbische Fischsuppe
Swabian Fish Soup

This dish, being directly related to the French version "Bouillabaisse," was adopted by the Swabians and – being as inventive as Swabians simply are – prepared with those ingredients available to them. The modern Swabian housewife surprises her loved ones with, for example, this recipe: For 4 persons allow for each: approx. 9 ounces yellow perch or pike and cod, halibut and salmon, 3½ ounces shrimps (in shell) and 9 ounces mussels. You will also need parsley, leek, carrots, at least 3 cloves garlic, 1 bouillon cube and 1 packet saffron.

Prepare stock as follows: Cook 2 quarts water, 1 bouillon cube, minced herbs, carrots and garlic.

Brush the mussels clean under running water and cook in stock over medium heat for 5 minutes.

Cut fish into small cubes, add to stock and simmer for 10 minutes in stock. Add

1 cup frozen (thawed) peas, shrimps and saffron to stock.
Bring to boil and garnish with fresh, chopped dill and chives.
Some insist that potatoes must be served with this dish, they are gravely mistaken. Fresh French bread is a tasty accompaniment.

Meat Dishes

("March of the Gaisburg People")

Gaisburger Marsch

Rindsrouladen

Beef Roulades or Rolls

This tasty meat dish requires some preparation in advance, however, it proves to be worth the effort later on at the table, due not only to the delicious meat, but also the gravy (very important to the Swabian).

Allow one roulade or roll per person. Have the butcher cut strips of aged hind shank. Ask him to take care that the strips are not cut too thinly. At home dry pieces of meat with paper towels. Spread one side of meat with mustard and then thinly with catsup. Place a strip of smoked bacon in the center of each strip and top with 1 tablespoon chopped onion and – if your taste buds so desire – anchovies or sliced dill pickles.

Fold over sides and roll, beginning with narrower end (rouler means rolling).

Fasten or tie with cotton thread, toothpicks or roulade needles, then season lightly with salt and pepper.

Brown the roulades, one after the other, in hot fat, on all sides. Then remove and set aside. Sauté in meat drippings 1 large onion, 1 tomato and parsley while stirring constantly. Add well-seasoned meat stock while stirring constantly. Then add the roulades and cook at low heat until tender.

To obtain a tasty gravy, brown a pig's forefoot (chopped) along with the roulades. Strain gravy through sieve and thicken with sour cream and a little flour (not more than 1 tablespoon).

Serve with "Spätzle," boiled potatoes or bread dumplings. Mashed potatoes and sweet-sour red cabbage are also tasty accompaniments. The tastiest treat for the Swabian is to dunk bread in the gravy leftover on his plate.

Fleischküchle
Swabian Hamburger Patties

If, while strolling by a Swabian butcher shop, you should notice the smell of freshly prepared "Fleischküchle," it is perfectly acceptable to give in to the temptation and eat one while on the run. "Fleischküchle" is, however, rather a sit-down dinner affair, served on weekdays with Swabian potato salad (recipe on page 124).

They're prepared as follows: Rub crust off 2 dry, day-old rolls and soak in hot water. Press excess water out of rolls and tear into small pieces. Combine the bread pieces with 1 minced onion and 1 bunch minced parsley and sauté in butter until soft. Let cool.

Then add to 18 ounces ground meat (pork and beef). Season with salt, pepper, nutmeg and add 2 eggs, mixing thoroughly. Shape into pocket-sized hamburger patties and fry in generous amount of fat until lightly browned on both sides.

Serve with potato salad as previously mentioned or, for a change, with a mixed potato and cucumber salad. Leftover "Fleischküchle" can be cut into slices and fried with scrambled egg or served with bread and mustard at "Vesper"-time (lunch served in the evening).

Laß mi' meine Küchle in dei'm Schmalz backe, no därfscht du dein Speck in mei'm Kraut kocha

(If you let me fry my patties in your bacon grease, I'll let you cook your bacon in my kraut)

Schwäbischer Rostbraten
Swabian Beefsteak

A Swabian "Rostbraten" is not merely a roasted piece of meat, it is moreover a nourishing affair.

Have your butcher cut not too thin slices of aged rib. The meat should be marbled with fat, since the fat keeps the steak tender during browning. Do not pound meat, however, slit the fatty edges with a knife.

Brown both sides of the "Rostbraten" in a generous amount of fat (for 3–4 minutes). Season well with pepper and salt. Reduce heat and cook for 5 minutes or longer, turning meat several times.

Place on heated plates and cover with aluminum foil.

Sauté thinly sliced onion rings in remaining pan drippings until lightly browned. Season with salt and layer on meat pieces. Serve with sauerkraut and "Spätzle" or tiny "Maultaschen" (recipe page 118). A Swabian "Trollinger" or "Schwarzriesling" (dry red wines) would accompany this dish excellently.

"Rostbraten" was never regarded as an economical dish, however, if properly prepared it is a sheer delicacy! An authentic "Rostbraten" should never be permitted to "hang over the edge of the plate," as some insist. For a Rostbraten the butcher will prepare slices from the original piece of meat, being approx. eight inches in length, slicing vertically. Therefore, the pieces should not be larger than 8 inches × 3 inches.

Schwäbischer Sauerbraten

Swabian Sweet-Sour Pot Roast

Ask your butcher for 35–53 ounces beef for "Sauerbraten" (rump or round). Marinade beef for 2–6 days in the following mixture: 1¼ cups wine vinegar (or dilute a sharp vinegar with wine), 1 tablespoon salt, several cloves and bay leaves, 6 or 7 peppercorns, 2 lemon slices, 1 medium-sized onion (sliced into rings), ½ leek leaf, 1 carrot and 1 small celery root (all diced), 1 tablespoon mustard seed and lastly 2½ cups sweet or sour milk or buttermilk.

The meat should be completely covered by the marinade. If not, turn frequently. (If you are in a hurry, however, at least 2 days in advance, bring marinade to a boil, let cool and soak meat in it.).

Now, here is how "Sauerbraten" is prepared: Remove meat from marinade and completely blot dry with paper towels. Brown in hot fat on all sides. Add fresh onion slices, parsley and 1 minced carrot and continue to brown. Pour some of the strained marinade stock and 1 bouillon cube over the meat.

Cover and simmer at low heat for approx. 1½–2 hours, adding additional marinade or water, if necessary.

Remove roast and set aside. Combine 1 tablespoon flour and ½ cup + 2 tablespoons sour cream and blend until smooth. Add to gravy stock, stirring constantly. Bring to a boil and strain. If desired, add additional sour cream, but do not reboil.

Serve with "Spätzle" or potato dumplings (made from cooked potatoes) and if desired, sweet-sour red cabbage. The ideal wine to be served with this dish would be a Swabian "Trollinger" or "Schwarzriesling" (dry red wines).

Zwiebelfleisch
Onion Roast

That Swabians are said to be penny-pinchers is not far-fetched. However, they save their pennies on the right things. "Zwiebelfleisch" is not prepared from scraps of meat, most definitely not. The flavor, the soup meat has been deprived of during cooking, is replaced during a second cooking process.

To prepare the soup combine soup vegetables, beef soup bones and a little water. Bring to a boil before adding soup meat (shank) and cook until tender. Then remove and cut into thin slices. Sauté in a pan thin onion slices in fat and add beef slices. Season with salt, pepper, garlic powder and continue to fry at high heat until well-browned while stirring constantly. Add additional fat if necessary and 1 or 2 well-beaten eggs.

Continue to cook until eggs are done. Serve with fried potatoes and a tossed green salad.

It might not be a bad idea to treat yourself to a “Magenbitter” or other German schnaps.

Bei de Reiche lernt m’r ’s Spare, bei de Arme ’s Koche

(The rich can teach you how to save, the poor how to cook)

Krautwickel
Stuffed Cabbage Rolls

Trim as many loose outer leaves from a head of green cabbage as are needed to stuff. Place leaves in a large bowl and pour boiling water over them. Then drain in colander. From remaining head of cabbage cut out stem and discard. Chop remaining cabbage into thin strips. Sauté 1 medium-sized onion in butter until light yellow in color and then add cabbage strips. Season with salt, pepper, paprika and nutmeg. While stirring constantly, continue to sauté for 5–10 minutes longer. Add ground meat and mix thoroughly. Place this mixture in center of well-drained cabbage leaves and fold over bottom edges first, then roll. Fasten with white cotton thread. Melt 1 tablespoon butter in a pan. Line bottom with thin strips of smoked bacon and place stuffed cabbage rolls closely together on top of bacon.

Brown, then pour beef stock or gravy

over top and simmer until tender at low heat, turning rolls and adding additional stock if necessary.

Stuffed cabbage rolls freeze well, therefore, why not prepare a few extra?

Kommet nach dem Kaffee, no könnet ihr zom Nachtessa wieder drhoim sei'

(Come on over to our house after the afternoon coffee has been served, so that you can leave in time to be back at home for dinner)

Kalbsnierenbraten

Rolled Roast Loin of Veal with Kidney

This is not exactly an economical dish, however, one can compensate by serving this roast thinly sliced and leftovers may be served cold, also thinly sliced on open-faced sandwiches or with potato salad. The easiest method of preparing this dish is to purchase a pre-rolled veal-kidney roast at the butcher's shop. The Swabian housewife, however, can only purchase 1 kidney roast and 1 veal kidney to match extra.

For 6 persons allow 54 ounces veal roast. Season well on all sides and place kidney on top. Roll tightly and fasten with thread as if wrapping a package. Brown on all sides in hot fat. Mince onion, 1 small carrot, 1 tomato and 1 slice celery root and add to roast while stirring constantly.

As soon as meat is browned, add approx. 1 tablespoon flour to pan drippings and cook, adding some water or stock. If desired add 1 bouillon cube. Bake in oven at 400 ° F (basting and turning often) for 1½ – 2 hours. Strain gravy and add some sweet cream for a smooth texture.

Serve roast slices with “Spätzle” and a tossed green salad.

Eingemachtes Kalbfleisch
Veal Stew

Back in the good old days when luxuries were rather scarce, this was a dish usually only served to women recently having given birth in order that they'd regain strength. (Swabians say: "Damit sie wieder auf d'Füß kamen." That means: So that they'd be able to get back on their feet.)

You will require 18–22 ounces veal breast (let your butcher know what you're preparing, so that he'll give you a thicker piece.) Cut in large pieces and pour boiling water over meat in order to attain a nice white color. Dry and brown in a pan, adding butter and 1 minced onion. Sprinkle 3 tablespoons flour over meat and add approx. 3 cups meat stock. Now add 1 onion stuck with 3 whole cloves, 2 bay leaves and 5–6 peppercorns. Also add 2 lemon slices (remove seeds) and salt.

Cover and simmer until tender. Lastly

add a sardine (cleaned under running water and minced), 3 tablespoons white wine and a shot lemon juice. Remove from heat. Combine 1 egg yolk and 2–3 tablespoons sour cream and stir until smooth. Add to gravy, stirring constantly. Add salt or bouillon cube. At this stage do not cook any longer.

Serve with "Spätzle" or rice. Even nowadays, "Eingemachtes Kalbfleisch" is a flavorful and tasty dish for persons adhering to a strict diet. However, healthy individuals enjoy this dish just as much (Swabians would say: "Aber es schmeckt au G'sonde guet.")

Siedfleisch
Soup Meat

"Siedfleisch mit Beilagen" (soup meat with a side dish) can often be spotted on the Swabian menu. A stranger cannot very well imagine what this dish is all about as opposed to the Viennese dish "Wiener Tafelspitz" (Viennese Tafelspitz). Both dishes consist of cooked beef. Ask your butcher for 27 ounces beef for cooking. He will provide you with either shank, short plate or brisket or, provided he knows that you prefer meat well-marbled with fat, rib roast. Also ask him for 3–4 soup bones (knuckles, shin bones). Combine and cook soup bones, coarsly-chopped leek, carrots, parsley and celery root in 1 quart water. Add 1 clove garlic, 1 tablespoon salt and 10 crushed peppercorns.

If you desire a nice clear stock, add the outer peeling of one onion.

Bring stock to a boil and add meat, then immediately reduce heat. The meat should simmer slowly for approx. 2 hours with pot only half-covered.

Slice meat as soon as it is tender and arrange on heated platter. Pour some of the hot stock over meat slices. This hot meat dish taken out of the "Sud" (stock) can be served with grated horseradish, beet salad and boiled potatoes or a potato-carrot mixture.

Some prefer to savor this dish with sweet-sour plum preserves or expensive cranberries. Others prefer to dunk the meat slices in salt and pepper and eat with a slice of hearty German country rye bread.

Gefüllte Kalbsbrust
Stuffed Breast of Veal

For this dish some planning in advance is required. Order 35 ounces breast of veal at the butcher's shop a day before butchering day, which should yield 4–6 servings and ask him to slit the pieces, so that they can be stuffed later. He will remove the bones and gristle and slit the sides to form pockets.

The stuffing is prepared as follows: Grate crusts off of 3 dry (day-old) rolls. Cut the remaining parts of the rolls into cubes and soak in 1¼ cups milk. Press out excess milk. Sauté moist bread cubes in 2 tablespoons butter, adding 1 minced onion, 1 tablespoon minced parsley and 1 mashed clove garlic.

Combine with 9 ounces ground meat, ½ cup less 1 tablespoon or 7 tablespoons "Bratwurstbrät" (special Swabian sausage dressing consisting of well-seasoned veal and pork). You may substitute with well-seasoned pork sausage, 2 egg yolks, a generous dash of salt and nutmeg. Beat egg whites until stiff and add to mixture. Rub veal pieces inside and out with salt and pepper, stuff with meat mixture and sew openings together with needle and cotton thread. Brown both sides of meat in fat in a casserole dish in oven. Add 1 carrot, 1 small onion, 1 tomato and 1 slice celery root (needed later on for gravy).

Bake at medium heat, basting often until crust is crispy brown. Combine pan drippings with some water and strain. Add some meat stock and sour cream and bring to a boil.

Slice and serve with – naturally – “Spätzle” (Swabian homemade noodles, recipe on page 14) and also “Ackersalat” (lamb’s lettuce).

This veal dish may also be served cold. Pistachios may be added to stuffing. Baking time: 1½ hours.

Gefüllte Kalbsbrust

Hohenloher Pfannenbrätle
Hohenloher Pan-Fry

This Sunday dish originates in the Frankish section of Germany, located between the Neckar and Tauber rivers. Drench thin slices of pork loin in flour and brown in a generous amount of fat. Beforehand, however, sauté fresh mushrooms and chanterelles - or even better yet, both types together, a peeled tomato (diced) in fat. Season to taste.

Arrange meat slices on heated platter, cover with mushroom mixture. Top with cooked asparagus and pour a Hollandaise sauce over everything.

Serve with homemade butter noodles, potato balls or – what a Swabian is not at all accustomed to eating, a tasty, light accompaniment - warm fresh white bread.

Innards

Kutteln
Tripe

Tripe or entrails, the first stomach of beef, is treasured in only a few parts of Germany, as in Swabia, also in France, Italy and Switzerland.

Purchase 18 ounces precooked tripe and ask the butcher to slice into thin strips.

Simmer, in order to obtain a dark sauce, 3½ tablespoons butter, 2 tablespoons flour and approx. 3¾ cups water.

Add bouillon cube, freshly ground pepper, 2 bay leaves, 3–5 cloves, 1 whole small onion und tripe slices. Cook 15–20 minutes until tender.

Season with either vinegar or red wine. Very often lately our menus in restaurants offer "Tripe in Calvados," which is not at all Swabian, however, very tasty. Serve with fried potatoes and a glass of red wine. As opposed to this sour tripe dish, another Swabian specialty is:

Geröstete Kutteln
Fried Tripe

Fry 1 small onion in butter until golden. Add cooked and sliced tripe. Cook for 20 minutes while stirring constantly. Season with salt and freshly ground pepper. Beat 2 eggs and pour over tripe. Cook only until done; no longer, or dish will become too dry.

Serve with a tossed green salad.

Kuttelsalat

Tripe Salad

Cook 18 ounces tripe (meaty part) until very tender and cut into thin strips. Pour the following (warm) marinade over tripe: vinegar, salt, pepper, dash sugar and minced onion.

Cook 1 cup yellow or red lentils in lightly salted water until tender. The lentils must remain whole and be slightly crisp, therefore, cook no longer than 10–15 minutes. Place lentils in colander and rinse with cold water. Drain well.

Add to tripe salad and mix well. If necessary, season with vinegar and salt. Sprinkle coarse freshly ground pepper over salad.

When arranged on lettuce leaves, you have an interesting entrée; when served with a slice of buttered bread, an ideal summertime meal.

Kalbsnierle
Veal Kidney

Clean 1 veal kidney under running water. Then dry and cut into thin slices. Slice onion into rings and sauté in fat until golden.

Add kidney slices and fry until no longer red in color.

Sprinkle flour over kidney mixture, add beef stock and cook for 10–15 minutes until tender. A bay leaf and clove should also be added before cooking.

Shortly before serving season with salt, pepper, sour cream and red wine or vinegar. Be careful not to add too much vinegar or wine, since the tasty kidney flavor may be lost.

Serve with fried potatoes, "Spätzle" or a slice of dark rye bread. A tossed salad goes well with this dish.

Gebackene Briesle

Baked Sweetbreads

Prepare 1 pair calf sweetbreads as follows: Soak in water for 2 hours, blanch shortly by pouring hot water over sweetbreads in order to obtain a nice white color. Weight them down between 2 moist wooden cutting boards and let cool (to crush fibers). When cooled, trim by removing cartilage, tubes, connective tissue and tougher membrane.

Slice into finger-sized slices, season with salt and pepper, drench in beaten egg and bread crumbs. Then fry in fat until golden brown. Serve with a tossed crispy salad if a hot luncheon dish is desired.

Back in the good old days, if a master craftsman was seen sitting in his favorite restaurant/tavern in the late afternoon, having ordered a "Trollinger-Viertele" (a glass of Swabian red wine) and "Briesle," you could be certain that he'd just finalized an important contract or received a payment due to him.

For "Briesle" was an expensive affair. Today it has come to be so "modern," that it is usually "all sold out."

**Das send rechte Leut',
die beim Schaffe frieret ond beim
Esse schwitzet!**

(Decent people are those who freeze while working and sweat during meals!)

Leberknödel

Liver Dumplings

You will need 13 ounces chopped liver (beef and pork), 3 eggs, 4 dry (day-old) rolls, salt, pepper, nutmeg, parsley and onion.

Cut 2 rolls into cubes and soak in hot water until soft.

Combine minced liver, salt, pepper, nutmeg and 3 eggs and mix well. Cut the remaining 2 rolls into very small cubes and add to liver mixture. This mixture must be allowed to rest in a cool place for at least 1/2 hour.

Drain the soaked rolls, press out excess liquid and tear into small pieces. Sauté in butter, adding minced onion and parsley, until transparent in color. Let cool. Then add to liver mixture and mix well.

Using a spoon dipped in water mold oval-shaped dumplings and drop into lightly salted boiling water. Lower heat and simmer for 8–10 minutes.

Now we have several serving alternatives:

Either we drop these dumplings, out of the "Sud" (stock) into beef stock and serve as a hearty soup or we fry them in butter and bread crumbs and serve with potato salad.
This luncheon dish will most certainly stave off hunger pains until the 6:00 p. m. evening bells ring ("dieses Mittagessen hält bestimmt vor bis zum 6-Uhr-Läuten").

Saures Herz

Heart in Sour Sauce

A day after butchering, the Swabian housewife usually ordered innards from the butcher: tripe, calf, beef, pork liver or a whole veal heart. Ordering in advance is today no longer necessary. Due to modern freezing equipment, innards can be purchased at the butcher's or supermarket on every weekday.

For a large veal heart prepare the following stock by combining: 7½ cups water, 1 tablespoon salt, a generous amount of green soup vegetables, 1 celery root, 1 carrot, 1 onion, 1 tablespoon tomato paste, approx. 5 crushed peppercorns and 1 clove garlic. Boil approx. 20 minutes. Clean heart under running water and remove all tubes and cartilage. Boil in stock until tender.

Sauté 1½ tablespoons butter or margarine, add 2–3 tablespoons flour and the strained stock while stirring constantly. Season with 1 dash sugar, 1 dash thyme and 1 dash ammonium carbonate, 2 tablespoons vinegar and a shot red wine. Cut heart into strips, drop into stock and bring to a boil.

Serve with boiled potatoes or "Spätzle."

Essa ond Trenka hält Leib ond Seel' zusammen

(Eating and drinking keeps body and soul in shape)

Hirnschnitten
Brain Slices

Brain slices are ideal when served alone for a late breakfast (brunch) or served with sautéed fresh mushrooms and a tossed green salad for an exquisite luncheon or dinner.

Soak 1 brain in water several times until freed of all traces of blood. Then soak in lukewarm water, skin and drain. Fry on all sides in butter, adding 1 minced onion. Soak 2 dry (day-old) rolls in milk, then press liquid out of rolls, tear into small pieces and combine with 2 well-beaten egg yolks. Season with salt and pepper and combine well with brain mixture. Generously spoon over slices of toast. Place under broiler for a few minutes.

Desserts

Hefezopf
Yeast Braid

A yeast braid must be prepared from a large amount of flour. Simply because the inside should be light and fluffy and the crust well-browned. When using less flour the inside becomes too dry. I am, however, certain that if you bake a large Swabian "Hefezopf," ready and willing eaters will automatically appear; particularly due to the pleasant aroma that will fill the whole house. Hefezopf also freezes well (after cooling).

Dissolve 2 ounces fresh yeast in 1/2 cup lukewarm milk, adding a dash of sugar. Place 14 cups flour in a bowl. Punch a well in the center and pour the dissolved yeast in it. Set aside and let rest in warm place. Beat until creamy 1 1/4 cups and 1 tablespoon butter and 1/2 cup and 2 1/2 tablespoons sugar.

Add grated rind and juice of one whole lemon and 1 teaspoon salt. Combine butter and flour mixtures, adding 5 cups lukewarm milk. Knead until air blisters appear under the surface. Place in a bowl, cover with cloth and let rest in a warm, draft-free place until doubled in bulk.

Then divide dough into 3 parts and roll into long sausage-shaped pieces. Braid, beginning in center and place on greased baking sheet. Set aside and let rest for a short period of time. Then brush with egg yolk and sprinkle with coarsly ground sugar and slivered almonds. A handful of raisins may be added during the first mixing stage.

Bake in a preheated oven at medium temperature until well-browned.

Hefezopf is delicious when eaten freshly baked, while still warm and served with a cup of coffee, however, it is not exactly easily digestible. It would actually be barbarian to dunk a piece of freshly baked Hefezopf into a hot drink. This is only permitted when it is dry and day-old.

Süße Quarkpfannkuchen
Sweet Ricotta Cheese Pancakes

Prepare 8 thin Flädle (pancakes/crêpes) according to recipe on page 114 and fry in only a little fat. Mix 18 ounces ricotta cheese with enough sugar to taste. Add as many raisins as desired and 4 egg yolks. Gently fold in 4 stiffly beaten egg whites.

Spread evenly on pancakes and roll.

Grease a casserole dish generously with butter and stack half of pancakes on bottom, the other half in the other direction on top. Dot with butter and – if it suits your taste buds – sprinkle with ground hazelnuts.

Bake in preheated oven for 30–40 minutes.

This dish is ideal for young and old sweettooths alike and healthy also. They also taste good when served cold.

Aufgezogene Dampfnudeln
Wound-Up Yeast Cakes

The song sung by children "Dampfnudeln ham'er gestern g'habt, Dampfnudeln ham'er heut" (yesterday we had Dampfnudeln, today we're having Dampfnudeln) actually is not Swabian, however, we enjoy this sweet treat on meatless days just as much.

First prepare a not too heavy yeast dough and let rise in a warm place until doubled in bulk. In a casserole dish heat 1 cup water, 1 tablespoon butter and a dash of salt. The water may be replaced by milk and the salt by 1 tablespoon sugar. Shape dough into coffee-cup-sized balls (oval-shaped) and place in heated liquid with sides touching. Cover with tight-fitting lid and simmer at low heat for 20–25 minutes. As soon as the bottoms are crusty brown remove and serve immediately.

Upon lifting the lid do not let the pale-faces staring back discourage you;

wound-up “Dampfnudeln” just are that way, since they are not baked – they’re wound-up in steam (therefore the name). Serve with stewed fruit or warm vanilla sauce.

M’r glaubt gar net, was älles in ein’ neigeht, wenn m’r eing’lade isch

(Hard to believe what can be packed into one’s belly when you’re a guest at someone else’s house)

Aufgezogene Dampfnudeln

Kirschenpfannkuchen
Cherry Pancakes

June 29th, St. Peter's and St.Paul's Day, is considered the peak day of the cherry season. One should take advantage of every opportunity of serving this flavorful fruit, which can be prepared in so many ways. Why don't you try cherry pancakes.

First you need 4 dry (day-old) rolls. Soak in water, press out excess liquid and pluck into small pieces. Add 4 tablespoons flour, 1 cup milk, 3 eggs, 2 tablespoons sugar, 1 teaspoon ground cinnamon and approx. 35 ounces pitted cherries (if possible dark, juicy cherries). Fry rather small pancakes in hot fat on both sides until lightly browned and sprinkle with sugar and cinnamon. For those who don't want to satisfy their appetite with only sweet dishes, serve a bowl of vegetable soup beforehand.

Rhabarberkuchen
Rhubarb Cake

In every Swabian garden or vineyard you will find one or two rhubarb bushes. In spring the housewife cuts 5 or 6 rhubarb stalks and conjours up a delicacy, which even sworn-in cake-haters can't turn down.

Combine 1¼ cups and 2 tablespoons flour, ½ cup and ½ tablespoon butter, 1 cup sour cream and knead quickly as for pie dough. Refrigerate for 1 hour. Roll the dough and line a round 10-inch (removable-rim pan) springform pan, being careful to line sides of pan all the way to top, so that the juicy rhubarb filling will not leak out. Prepare filling as follows: Peel rhubarb stalks and dice into ¾–1 inch pieces. To soften, blanch by pouring hot water over pieces, then drain.

Sprinkle generously with sugar and fill evenly into pie shell. For topping combine 1¼ cups sweet cream, 2–3 tablespoons flour, 3 egg yolks and 1/2 cup and 2 1/2 tablespoons sugar and beat until creamy. Beat remaining egg whites until stiff and gently fold into egg yolk mixture. Spread over pie shell and bake in preheated oven for approx. 35 minutes.

Essa ond Trenka hält Leib ond Seel' zsamma

(Eating and drinking keeps body and soul in shape)

Streuselkuchen
Streusel Cake

This rather pale-looking baked concoction releases its deliciousness already during the first bite. Should you notice slight stomach trouble later on, it is because one just couldn't resist devouring a piece of warm cake fresh out of the oven, instead of waiting until cooled. (So hat man's halt mal wieder "nicht verheben" können, ein Stück frisch aus dem Backofen, bevor der Kuchen ganz erkaltet war, zu naschen.) Prepare Streuselkuchen as follows: Combine 18 ounces flour, 3/4 oz. fresh yeast, 1/2 cup less 1 tablespoon butter, 3 1/2 tablespoons sugar, 2 eggs, lemon rind of 1 lemon, dash lemon juice, 1 1/4 cups milk, 1/2 tablespoon lard and beat well. Cover and let rest in warm, draft-free place. Once doubled in bulk, roll dough and line a generously-greased oblong baking sheet. Let rise again for a short period of time. Prick the lower crust with a fork and brush with melted butter.

For the last step prepare streusel as follows: Combine 1/2 cup less 1 tablespoon butter, 1/2 cup less 1 tablespoon sugar, 3/4 cup less 1 tablespoon flour, 1 small package chopped almonds (approx. 1/4 cup) and 1/2 teaspoon ground cinnamon. Blend until these ingredients crumble. Before sprinkling over cake, refrigerate for a short period of time.

Flachswickel

Tiny-Braided Yeast Coffee-Cakes

This is a very rich yeast cake, ideal to be served with the afternoon cup of coffee or on Sunday morning.

Combine 1 cup and 1 tablespoon butter (beaten until creamy), 2 eggs (room temperature), dash salt, 18 ounces flour, 1 ounce fresh yeast dissolved beforehand in a little (approx. 1/4 cup) warm milk and 1 teaspoon sugar and permitted to rest for 10 minutes. Mix well and knead until smooth and elastic. Roll dough until shaped like a long sausage and slice into 1-inch-pieces. Using hands, roll each of these pieces into 4-inch-strips. Drench pieces in coarse sugar or – even better yet – in a mixture of sugar and cinnamon. Then braid all of the strips (3-plait) into small coffee cakes and place on well-greased baking sheet.

Cover with towel and let rise in warm place for approx. 30–45 minutes. Brush with beaten egg yolk ("verkleppertem Eigelb") and bake at medium heat for 30 minutes until lightly browned.

You will most definitely be able to impress your guests at your next afternoon coffee hour. The unbaked coffee cakes freeze well. Simply thaw and bake in oven.

Schneckennudeln
Yeast Cinnamon Buns or Snails

For these famous Swabian sweet rolls, being the size and shape of a saucer, prepare yeast dough, or better yet, for beginners, purchase ready-made yeast dough. Prepare according to package directions. After first rising roll into an 8 inches by 16 inches rectangle. Brush with melted butter and sprinkle with a handful of washed and dried raisins and currants and sugar and cinnamon (6 parts sugar to 1 part cinnamon). Then roll the dough like a jelly roll beginning with the narrower end (not too tightly). Using a sharp knife cut into 1 inch slices (not larger) and place each slice or roll (cut-sides touching baking sheet) on well-greased baking sheet, being careful not to place too closely together, since they will expand.

Cover with towel and let rise in warm place. Brush with beaten egg yolk.

Bake these "Schneckennudeln" in a preheated oven on rack placed in center of oven at medium heat. While still warm spread with a lemon glaze, which you have prepared during the baking stage, as follows: Combine 1 cup powdered sugar, 1 tablespoon water and 2 tablespoons lemon juice and cook until transparent in color ("zum Faden kochen").

Using a pastry brush spread glaze over the "Schneckennudeln" while they're still warm. The glaze adds flavor and provides a decorative touch.

Grießschnitten
Farina Slices

"Grießschnitten" can be prepared for sweettooths as well as for those who prefer a saltier version. The base, the farina pudding, is the same for both versions.
Combine 5 cups milk, 3½ tablespoons butter, a dash salt, grated lemon rind of one whole lemon and 1¾ cups farina and cook into a very stiff pudding (as soon as it begins to thicken lower heat, since it burns easily).
Let cool. Beat 2–3 eggs and add, mixing thoroughly. If the sweet version is desired add 2 tablespoons sugar.
Spread pudding into a moistened baking dish using a spatula to spread evenly.
Once thoroughly cool, cut into diamond, square or rectangular shaped pieces and fry in generous amounts of fat until golden brown.
Another version: The cut-out pieces may be breaded by dipping into beaten egg and drenched in bread crumbs, and then fried.

For the sweet version sprinkle with sugar and cinnamon mixture. Serve with canned fruit (sour cherries are especially tasty). For the salty version serve with a bowl tossed green or chef's salad. Some people actually - not only Swabians - order a serving of juicy potato salad to go along with this dish.

Apfelküchle
Apple Cakes

The first step is to prepare a beer batter combining 1¾ cups flour, 1¼ cups beer, 1 tablespoon oil, a dash salt, 1 tablespoon sugar and 4 egg yolks and beat until batter is of a medium consistency. Beat remaining egg whites until stiff and gently fold into batter.

Then peel and core 4 tart apples of same size (the varieties ripe earliest in the year are definitely suitable for this dish, e. g. Greenups or Transparents). Slice into ½–1-inch-rings and sprinkle with lemon juice, also rum or arrack and lastly sugar. Drench apple slices lightly in flour and dip into batter. Fry in a generous amount of fat until golden brown. While hot sprinkle with cinnamon and sugar mixture.

Serve with vanilla dessert sauce, wine custard or simply with a hot cup of coffee. Back in the good old days, "Apfelküchle" were considered a complete meal on “meatless” days. Nowadays, the housewife will most certainly receive lots of praise from her guests if she serves them as a dessert. There’s always room for an “Apfelküchle” (Ein Apfelküchle geht immer noch “nonder”).

Pfitzauf

Egg Soufflé or Timbales

In order to prepare this dish you will require a special mold: an earthenware, ovenproof, straight-sided dish, in which 6 soufflés can be baked at the same time. Such a mold can be purchased in any reputable Swabian household goods store.

For 2×6 soufflés combine 2½ cups and 1 tablespoon flour and 3¾ cups milk and blend well. Beat 3½ tablespoons sugar and 5 eggs and add to the flour-milk mixture, stirring well. Lastly, add 7 tablespoons melted butter. Stir well and pour into the well-greased (with butter) soufflé molds, however, only half-full; better yet, not quite half-full, as these soufflés will greatly expand (stark "aufpfitzen"). Bake in oven at medium temperature until golden brown, being careful not to open oven door during the beginning stage of baking.

Remove Pfitzauf from molds while still hot and sprinkle with powdered sugar.

Serve with whipped cream and coffee or stewed fruit or a vanilla dessert sauce. The sugar in the dough may be omitted and once the pastry has cooled, you may slice open and fill with a frozen cream-horseradish sauce.

Butter-S

Butter S-Shaped Cookies

Butter-S are not cut out, the Swabian housewife shapes them by hand. Each of these S-shaped Christmas cookies ("Weihnachtsgutsle") must be equal in size.

Ingredients: 3½ cups flour, 1 cup and 1 tablespoon butter, ½ cup and 1 tablespoon sugar, 7 egg yolks or 3 whole eggs.

For 80–100 Butter-S ("Essle"), quickly work dough with hands on a wooden pastry board until smooth. Then let rest in refrigerator. You may refrigerate overnight, thus dividing work over a period of two days (busy working individuals will welcome this idea).

Cut dough into 2–3 parts and shape with hands (roll) into tiny sausage-shaped pieces (1–1¼ inches thick), shape into an S and place on well-greased cookie sheet. Brush with stiffly-beaten egg white and sprinkle generously with coarse sugar. Bake at medium heat until golden brown.

Other types of Christmas cookies may be prepared using margarine, however, Butter-S ("Butter-Essle") must be prepared with butter.

Kommet nach dem Kaffee, no könnet ihr zom Nachtessa wieder drhoim sei'

(Come on over to our house after the afternoon coffee has been served, so that you can leave in time to be back at home for dinner)

Ausstecherle

Cut-Out Cookies

The most popular Christmas cookie is "Ausstecherle." Children especially enjoy these because they're cut into merry shapes such as pigs, hearts, butterflies, half-moons and mushrooms.

Cookie cutters can be purchased in any household goods store.

Ingredients for dough are: 3½ cups flour, 1 cup + ½ tablespoon butter, ½ cup + 2½ tablespoons to 1 cup + 1 tablespoon sugar, 3–4 whole eggs and a generous amount lemon rind. (Yields 90–100 cookies.) Sift flour, combine with other ingredients and work lightly with fingertips (or use a pastry blender and work dough in chopping motion for even better results). Dough must be allowed to rest in a cold place for 1 hour or wrap in aluminum foil and refrigerate. Using knife, cut into 2–3 parts and roll into oblong to approx. ⅕ inch thickness.

Be careful to roll evenly and not thicker

than 1/5 inch, otherwise “Ausstecherle” will not all brown to the same extent, nor will they taste or look alike.

Cut shapes out of dough with cookie cutters; scraps of dough should be rolled again.

Brush cookies with beaten egg yolk. You may sprinkle with coarse sugar or slivered or sliced almonds or colored sugar.

Bake on rack placed in center of oven for 5–10 minutes until golden. These thin cookies bake to a crisp very quickly. Therefore, pay attention at all times, since a whole baking sheet of cookies (“Gutsle”) may be burnt.

After cooled, layer into cookies tins.

Albertle
Rolled Butter Cookies

The Swabian is familiar with a broad assortment of Christmas cookies or "Gutsle." The Swabian housewife doesn't mind the work involved in delighting her loved ones with her baking talent during the holiday season. You are already familiar with "Butter-S" ("Essle," recipe page 97), "Ausstecherle" (Cut-out Cookies, page 99), and now "Albertle." The recipe being as follows: 3½ cups flour, 1 cup and 1 tablespoon sugar, 4 eggs, ½ cup and ½ tablespoon butter. 1½ cups corn starch, 3 tablespoons sweet cream, 1 tablespoon baking powder and 1 teaspoon vanilla extract.

First of all, beat butter until creamy and add all other ingredients in parts, setting ¾ cup less 1 tablespoon of the flour aside. Quickly work dough with hands on wooden pastry board, adding the remaining flour.

Permit dough to rest in cold place for 1 hour, then roll into a thin oblong and press grater on top of dough, leaving an interesting imprint in dough (finest grating part). Cut into tiny squares or use cookie cutters.

Bake on well-greased cookie sheet until golden.

By the way, "Albertle" are not Christmas cookies exclusively. Doting mothers of small children used to bake them the whole year through. Today, cookie production companies have relieved mothers of this chore.

Ofenschlupfer
Bread Pudding

Thinly slice 5–6 rolls. Sweeten to taste approx. 2½ cups milk, pour over slices and let soak.

In the meantime, peel and dice 18 ounces very ripe apples. Cook adding a little water, sugar and a dash cinnamon. Simmer until soft.

Layer, alternating with parts of soaked roll slices, chopped almonds, washed raisins and cooked apples into a well-greased casserole dish or mold. The top layer must consist of roll slices.

Pour over top a well-beaten mixture of 2 eggs, a little milk and sugar to taste. Dot top generously with butter.

Bake at relatively high heat for 1 hour until lightly browned and crispy.

Serve with vanilla-milk (heated milk, adding vanilla bean and a little sugar) or stewed fruit. A tasty accompaniment is also a cup of good coffee.

Ofenschlupfer

"Oven Crawler")

Schwarzwälder Kirschtorte
Black Forest Cherry Cake

For the original version of the Black Forest Cherry Cake only sour cherries may be used.

Ingredients for the cake layers: 1/2 cup + 2 1/2 tablespoons butter, 1/2 cup + 2 1/2 tablespoons sugar, 4 eggs, approx. 1/2 cup + 2 tablespoons milk, 3 1/2 ounces dark chocolate shavings, 1 3/4 cups flour, 1 teaspoon baking powder.

Ingredients for filling: 27 ounces pitted sour cherries, 3 tablespoons sugar, 5–10 tablespoons "Schwarzwälder Kirschschnaps" (cherry schnaps), 3 3/4 cups whipped cream (stabilized with 1 tablespoon dissolved gelatin and sweetened with 2–3 tablespoons sugar). For decoration of completed torte:

1 3/4 ounces chocolate shavings. To prepare layers beat butter until creamy, add sugar, egg yolks, milk and chocolate shavings. Sift and add gradually the flour and baking powder. Lastly, gently fold in the

stiffly-beaten egg whites. Bake in a well-greased and floured 10-inch-springform-pan (removable-rim pan) at medium heat until golden in color. (Torte layers of a good quality may also be purchased ready-made). Sprinkle sugar over cherries and set aside for several hours. Let cake layer cool and slice into 3 layers. Sprinkle bottom layer with "Kirschwasser," place drained cherries closely together on cake layer and spread some whipped cream on top. Sprinkle the second layer with the remaining strained cherry juice and spread some whipped cream on layer. Top with third layer, spread top and sides with remaining whipped cream and garnish with chocolate shavings.

"Schwarzwälder Kirschtorte" is a whipped cream-type pastry which men also appreciate, since the sour cherries and liqueur add a tangy, "masculine touch."

Rote Grütze
Red Berry Dessert Mold

During the peak season, when fresh berries are available, many a person may feel it a shame that these refreshing fruit dishes cannot be prepared during the colder months. "Rote Grütze" can, however, be prepared by using frozen berries.

Combine in saucepan 18 ounces red currants (Träuble, Johannisbeeren), 9 ounces raspberries, 3/4 cups + 2 tablespoons to 1 cup + 1 tablespoon sugar and 2 1/2 cups water. Cook until soft and then strain through sieve. Add additional water to obtain 5 cups of this fruit juice.

Stir 1/2 cup and 1 1/2 tbsp. (9 1/2 tbsp.) cornstarch into 1/4 of fruit juice. Bring remaining fruit juice to a boil. Add thickened juice to boiling juice, stirring constantly. Simmer for 5 minutes.

Pour into a mold that has been rinsed with cold water.

The cornstarch may be substituted by tapioca or farina, however, do not use less than 1/2 cup and 1 1/2 tablespoons. To add a special touch, 1 3/4 ounces ground almonds may be added to the mixture while warm.

Invert mold and serve either with a vanilla sauce or whipped cream (beaten only until half-stiff). If you decide to serve both, no one will complain. Garnish with the most appealing fresh berries, which were set aside.

Kirschenmichel
Cherry Soufflé

During the cherry season, this healthy dish, which children especially enjoy, is served on meatless days.

Combine 6 egg yolks and 1 cup + 1 tablespoon sugar until creamy. Grate rind off of 4–6 dry (day-old) rolls and add to egg-yolk mixture. Beat 6 egg whites until stiff and gently fold in. Combine 35 ounces pitted sour cherries with 3½ ounces slivered almonds and spike with a "Gläschen" (shot glass) kirschwasser (cherry schnaps). Pour into a well-greased (butter) casserole dish. If desired, add lemon rind and cinnamon. Pour egg-yolk mixture on top. Bake in preheated oven (350 °F). Position on rack in oven so that dish can expand in height. Bake 50–60 minutes until golden, crispy brown.

To make more appealing to the eye, sprinkle powdered sugar over top. Can also be eaten cold.

Wer satt ist, dem schmecket alle Kirschen sauer

(Those with a full belly will insist that all cherries taste sour)

What the Swabian Especially Enjoys Eating

Saure Kartoffelrädle
Sour Potato Stew

In other parts of Germany, this dish is also known as Brown Potato Stew.

You will need: 35 ounces boiled "kleine Kartoffeln" (small potatoes cooked in their jackets). Peel and slice into "Rädle" (thin slices).

Sauté 3–4 tablespoons flour in 3–3½ tablespoons fat, stirring constantly to obtain a sauce starter. As soon as light yellow in color, add 1 whole minced onion and simmer.

Once the desired coloring has been attained, add approx. 5 cups well-seasoned meat stock or bouillon broth, stirring well.

Then add 3 tablespoons vinegar, 1–2 bay leaves, 2 cloves and several peppercorns. Simmer for approx. 20–25 minutes, while stirring often. Cover with tightly fitting lid.

Press through sieve and add ½ cup white or red wine, ½ teaspoon marjoram (oregano) and additional salt if desired.

Carefully add sliced potatoes, return to stove plate, but do not cook.
Those who cannot watch calories may eat a slice of “Schwarzbrot” (dark German rye bread) along with this dish.

Flädle

Thin Pancakes/Crêpes

"Flädle" are thin pancakes, which Swabians incorporate into dishes in the most appetizing manner.

To prepare, you will require: 1 cup and 1/2 tablespoon flour, 2 eggs, 1 1/4 cups milk, dash of each: salt and nutmeg. Combine and blend until smooth. Let rest for 30 minutes.

Peel an onion, cut in half, skewer rounded side onto fork, dip flat side of onion in fat (butter, oil or margarine) and use to grease skillet. Pour only a small quantity of batter into skillet, so that by skillfully tipping the skillet, the batter will only thinly coat the bottom. The same Viennese rule applying to apple strudel (one should be able to read a newspaper through the paper-thin dough) also applies to Swabian "Flädle." Roll, thinly slice (look like noodles) and serve by pouring meat stock over sliced "Flädle." Or spread with filling. Several fillings are possible. I would like to introduce you to two: a salty and a sweet version.

Salty version: Combine ground meat, egg, sautéed onion and green vegetables (parsley, leek, chives). Spread on "Flädle" and roll. Place closely together in a well-greased casserole dish and brown until done.

Sweet version: Prepare filling by combining cottage cheese (pressed through sieve or processed in blender) or ricotta cheese, eggs, sugar, lemon rind and raisins (soaked in alcohol). Spread on "Flädle" and roll. These are also placed closely together in a well-greased casserole dish and browned until crispy.

These are only two of the many possible versions. The Swabian housewife uses her imagination to create 10 additional versions.

Linsen und Spätzle

Lentil Stew and Spätzle or Noodles

"Linsen" (lentils) belong to the family of legumes, which our ancestors were introduced to by the Romans. They are the absolute favorite of the Swabian, especially when served with the native "Spätzle."

Wash approx. 9 ounces lentils in cold water several times and soak in pot overnight. Water should cover lentils by approx. 1 inch.

The next day add additional water to the tenderized lentils, 1 bay leaf and approx. 9 ounces lean bacon rind. Cook until lentils are tender but not mushy. Prepare a sauce starter by browning butter or margarine and flour (see Sour Potato Stew, page 112). Add a little water and the lentil mixture.

Season with salt, pepper and a bouillon cube and bring to a rapid boil.

Lastly, season with vinegar. Either dice bacon rind or slice and serve alongside.

Last of all an important addition: It would be impossible to serve this dish without "Saitenwürstle" (sausages similar to frankfurters). Heat sausages in boiling water for 10 minutes. Now the picture is complete, with which, years ago, a sense of "Aushausigkeit" (wastefulness) was documented: "Heut gibt's Lensa ond Spätzle, mit Rauchfleisch und Saita garniert." (Today we're having "Linsen" and "Spätzle" served with bacon and sausages.)

Maultaschen

Meat Pockets, Similar to Kreplach, Won Ton Soup or Ravioli Squares

According to the motto "what you don't see is not there," generations ago, "Maultaschen" were an ideal dish for the pharisees during the fasting period. To make a long story short, meat ingredients were hidden in noodle dough.

Prepare a noodle dough by kneading 3½ cups flour, 3 eggs and salt or purchase ready-made dough from the bakery (must be ordered in advance).

Cut dough into 8 inch by 10-inch-strips and spread with the following delicious filling: 7 ounces cold roast or ground meat, 3½ ounces bacon or Bologna-type sausage, 3½ ounces "Brät" (substitute with pork sausage, refer to page 25) and 4 dry (day-old, soaked in water) rolls. Put these ingredients through meat grinder. Then add 4 eggs, salt, pepper and nutmeg.

Sauté 1 tablespoon each of chopped parsley, minced onion in 1½ tablespoons fat.

Let cool. Add to ground meat mixture. Then add 18 ounces cooked, well-strained and finely chopped spinach. Thoroughly mix and check seasoning once more. Spread evenly on strips of dough. Roll strips and cut into rectangular pieces or squares.

Drop the completed "Maultaschen" into salted boiling water and cook for 8 – 10 minutes.

Three serving alternatives are possible: Serve as soup in meat stock or broth and cover with "geschmälzter" onion (minced onion sautéed in fat), or "geschmälzten" bread crumbs, or serve with potato salad, or cut into thin strips, fry in butter and cover with beaten egg mixture until done and serve with a tossed green salad and potato salad.

Sometimes the humorous Swabians make a real "Maultaschen"-festival with this dish by first serving them in broth and then "geschmälzt" with salad.

Bob Larson informed Americans living in "Schwabenland" as follows: A high-caloric Swabian dish is "Maultaschen." Actually, the word-for-word translation would be "snout pockets." They look like giant ravioli squares; however, they are prepared and served in a different manner. Some say there are as many different "Maultaschen"-recipes as there are Swabian housewives. Many Americans first meet "Maultaschen" when they're swimming in broth, however, there are many different versions of this dish.
(Bob Larson, "Your Swabian Neighbors")

“Buabaspitzle” oder Schupfnudeln
“Boys’ Penises” or Potato Noodles

Peel 35 ounces potatoes (boiled in jackets the day before) and rice by putting through food mill, ricer or strainer or grate.

Combine with 2 whole eggs, 1 teaspoon salt and generous amount nutmeg, adding only as much flour as is needed until dough is no longer moist. Shape on floured surface into a thick roll, approx. 1 1/2 inches in diameter.

Cut into 3/4 inch thick slices and shape – also on floured surface – using fingers of both hands into 2 – 2 1/4 inch long (both ends pointed) “Buabaspitzle.” Drop into lightly salted, boiling water and simmer (do not boil).

As soon as they rise to surface, remove with slotted spoon and drain.

Let dry on a towel or platter.

Once cooled, fry these “Buabaspitzle” in a pan adding fat until golden and serve with a mixed tossed salad or directly out of the “Sud” (boiling liquid) “nacket” (naked) as an accompaniment to “Sauerbraten” (Sweet-Sour Pot Roast).

The artist of the “Der arme Poet” (Poor Poet), the native Bavarian, Carl Spitzweg, particularly enjoyed Swabian “Buabaspitzle.”

Buabaspitzle

Schwäbischer Kartoffelsalat
Swabian Potato Salad

This accompaniment to a roast or "Bratwurst" (broiled or frying sausage), "Fleischküchle" (fried meat patties) and "Leberkäs" (baked veal loaf) is often verbally downgraded, however, deep down passionately loved. Many hefty discussions have been carried on concerning its preparation. There is, however, only one method of preparation:

Never add: sour apple slices, fried bacon, pickles or possibly even mayonnaise. The only authentic preparation method is as follows: purchase firm-cooking potatoes (small, red, waxy potatoes). Swabians use "Sieglinde" or the small "Mäusle," harvested in spring. Make sure that all potatoes are of the same size to ensure appealing "Rädle" (slices). Boil potatoes in their jackets in salted water or in a pressure cooker. Peel while still warm and cut into thin slices.

Top with 1 minced onion, some salt,

pepper, not too much vinegar and lastly, warm seasoned meat broth.

Toss gently using salad servers, cover and let rest for at least 1 hour in warm place. Then add generous amount of oil and toss gently. Let marinate for a while and sprinkle with minced fresh chives.

“Kartoffelsalat” is a success if it slurps/ glides from the spoon (“quietscht”) while serving.

Salzkuchen
Salt Cake or Sour Cream Quiche

For those who do not care to bake a "Salzkuchen," this cake may be sampled time and time again at numerous country festivals and at the "Kirbe" or "Kirchweih" (church festival). Our country ladies set up their stands and offer this Swabian speciality hot out of the oven.

The recipe: Combine 1 cup and 6 tablespoons flour, 4 1/2 tbsp. fat (lard tastes best), dash salt and 1/2 cup milk and knead as for pie dough. Refrigerate for at least 1/2 hour. Roll and line a well-greased baking sheet with dough. Prepare topping as follows: Combine 2 cups sour cream, 3 egg yolks, salt and caraway seed and beat with whisk until smooth. Spread on top of dough, dot with butter pieces and generous amount of fresh, minced chives. Bake for approx. 1/2 hour. This cake should be eaten while still hot. Why not enjoy with a glass of Swabian wine (new wine would also be fine), which is the ideal accompaniment. In some parts of the country this cake is known as “Dai” or “Daie” and is ideal for the person who does not dare try a piece of Swabian onion cake.

Ein voller Bauch
lobt das Fasten

(A full belly praises the art of fasting)

Zwiebelkuchen
Onion Cake or Quiche

Every authentic Swabian household prepares "Zwiebelkuchen" once a year, in fall, when the new onions are juiciest and mild in flavor, creating this typical delicacy. During the same time of the year the "Federweiße" (feather-white) or "Räße" (new wine, slightly sour) is available, which is an ideal accompaniment to "Zwiebelkuchen."

To prepare "Zwiebelkuchen" prepare a yeast dough by combining 1¾ cups flour, 4½ tablespoons lard, ½ teaspoon salt, ½ ounce fresh yeast, milk or water. Knead, let rise and roll. Line baking sheet with dough, pinching up sides to form edge.

To prepare filling: Peel 35 ounces onions, cut into thin slices, combine with 4 tablespoons chopped bacon and sauté in fat until soft, being careful that onions do not change color. Let cool.

Combine 5½ tablespoons flour with

$1^1/_4$ cups sour cream. Add the onion mixture, 3 to 4 eggs, 1 level teaspoon salt and 1 tablespoon caraway seed. Stir until smooth and spread on dough. Dot with butter pieces and bake at medium to high heat until golden brown.

Swabian Zwiebelkuchen must be served warm. Leftovers may, however, be slowly reheated in oven.

Gurkengemüse

Cucumber Stew

Now you will experience an unusual hot vegetable dish, which is very tasty and also, in summer, very economical. Peel one large cucumber and cut in two lengthwise. Remove seeds with spoon. Slice the two halves into 1/3-inch-pieces. Now sauté 2–3 tablespoons minced onion in 3 1/2 tablespoons butter until light yellow in color, while stirring constantly. Add cucumber slices, cover and simmer over medium heat for 10 minutes. Then add a little granulated bouillon, 1/2 cup and 2 tablespoons sour cream, and, if necessary, only a little water. Cover and simmer until tender.

Before serving add generous amount of fresh, chopped dill. This spicy vegetable dish may be served with noodles or white rice.

If desired, you may dilute this dish with water and serve as soup, in which case each serving is topped with 1 extra tablespoon sour cream. Tastes good served with a piece of "Bauernbrot" (hearty country rye bread).

Zum Tisch gehört meh' als bloß a weißes Tischtuch

(A table needs more than just a white tablecloth)

Saure Flädle

Sour Pancake Strips

This is a superb version of "Saure Kartoffelrädle" (Sour Potato Stew - page 112) and is often served on Fridays. This dish most definitely is not a poor-man's dinner ("Armeleute-Essen"), it is rather a genuine delicacy.

First, prepare pancake batter by combining 1 cup + 1/2 tablespoon flour, 2 eggs, 1 1/4 cups milk, dash each of salt and nutmeg. Fry into very thin crêpes. Let cool. Then roll and cut into very thin strips.

Then prepare the "saure Brühe" (sour broth) as follows: Brown 3–3 1/2 tablespoons fat and 3–4 tablespoons flour, stirring constantly. As soon as the mixture is light yellow in color, add 1 minced onion and sauté. As soon as the mixture has attained the desired color, add 5 cups well-seasoned meat broth (or bouillon broth), 3 tablespoons vinegar, 1–2 bay leaves, 2 cloves and several peppercorns.

Cover and simmer for 20–25 minutes,

while stirring constantly. Strain and add ½ cup white or red wine, ½ teaspoon oregano, and, if desired, extra salt. Add the thinly-sliced crêpes carefully. Return to stove, however, do not bring to a boil.

Kässpätzle

Cheese "Spätzle" or Cheese Noodles

This dish must be well-prepared since it becomes cold quickly. Using a slotted spoon, remove either packaged or homemade noodles, or "Spätzle" prepared with a special noodle press (for recipe see page 14) from boiling water and drain in colander. Layer, alternating on heated serving platter noodles, generous amount of grated cheese (Swiss, Parmesan or Gouda) and butter pieces. Before serving sauté minced onion and bacon in fat, season with freshly-ground pepper and spread over top of dish.

Serve with a tossed salad.

Once you've eaten two servings of "Kässpätzle" you've had enough (Swabian: "dann battet's").

Schwäbischer Wurstsalat
Swabian Sausage Salad

Slice equal parts of "Schinkenwurst" (light-colored Bologna-type sausage made of pork and ham), "weiße Preßwurst" (white sausage, made of pork, incl. brawn or head cheese), and "Schwartenmagen" (head cheese) or "Schwarzwurst" (blood sausage) into thin strips or cubes.

Prepare dressing by combining wine vinegar (or vinegar diluted with wine), salt, pepper and a dash sugar (be generous with coarse pepper.) Pour over sausage strips and let marinate.

Either chop 1 onion or cut into thin rings, add to salad and pour very little oil over top.

Serve with fried potatoes or slices of rye bread and light beer. A fresh bread pretzel is also a tasty accompaniment.

Upon having consumed "ein Viertele zuviel am Abend zuvor" (one glass wine too much the night before), "Wurstsalat" is ideal to get one's stomach back to normal.

What the Swabian also Enjoys Eating

Krautspätzle

Cabbage "Spätzle" or Cabbage Noodles

Combine very dry sauerkraut, several tablespoons lard and 1 large onion and brown in a cast-iron pan while stirring constantly. Season to taste with salt, pepper and crushed juniper berries.

In the meantime prepare "Spätzle" (recipe page 14) and layer into a heated deep bowl, alternating with "Kraut" and "Spätzle." Brown minced onion in fat (preferably lard or lard with cracklings) and sprinkle over top.

This is one of the many versions including the Swabian special noodle "Spätzle." A glass of "Most-Schorle" (mixed drink of cider and soda water) could possibly help the liver digest the lard more easily.

Schwarzwurzel in Pfannkuchenteig

Scorzonera in Pancake Dough

(or substituted by oyster plant)

Years ago, scorzonera was referred to as "poor man's" asparagus. Over the years, lesser amounts are being planted. Most prefer asparagus because the higher price no longer hurts the pocketbook and because more work is required in preparing scorzonera. The dark peeling must be completely removed beforehand. Scrub under running water and scrape peeling off with knife.

Then slice into pieces 3–4 inches in length and place in a bowl filled with a solution of vinegar, water and 1 tablespoon water (to prevent pieces from turning dark). Cook pieces in the following broth until tender: lightly-salted water, 1 cup milk. Drain and blot dry with paper towel. Dunk the pieces in a very stiff pancake batter and fry in hot fat until golden brown.

This protein-rich vegetable dish, also recommended for diabetics, may be served with a mixed salad.

Certain Swabian “specialists” prefer scorzonera instead of asparagus due to the stronger flavor.

Scorzonera may well be served with a glass of “Schwarzriesling” (dry red Swabian wine).

Geröstete Kartoffeln mit Leberwurst

Fried Potatoes with Liver Sausage

This is one of the simple, however, tasty Swabian dishes, which, for example, is delicious when served after a long walk in the woods or after an afternoon of hard work in the "Güetle" (yard or garden). Potatoes boiled in their jackets the day before are required. Peel and cut into "Rädle" (thin slices). Brown minced onion in lard, add potato slices and fry, stirring constantly, until golden brown. Season with salt, pepper and oregano. Then add a "Hausmacher- oder Schlachtplatten-Leberwurst" (liver sausages) – remove skin beforehand and cut into small pieces – to potato mixture and mix well. If portions and appetite coincide, no accompaniment is necessary, however, a large bowl of tossed salad would do just fine.

Laubfröschle

Foliage Frogs or Stuffed Spinach

Remove stems from 20 large spinach leaves and blanch by pouring hot water over them. Then drain each on kitchen towels. Soak two dry (day-old) rolls, squeeze excess water out and pluck into small pieces. Mince 1 onion and 1 bunch parsley and sauté in 2 tablespoons butter. Let cool and combine with 2 eggs and 9 ounces "Bratwurstbrät" (Swabian sausage dressing consisting of veal, pork and spices. You may substitute with well-seasoned pork sausage, refer to page 25). Mix well. Then add generous amounts of nutmeg and pepper, and a little salt. Melt butter in a casserole dish. Then spread meat mixture on spinach leaves and place in casserole with even sides facing upwards. Pour a little meat or bouillon stock over spinach rolls. Cover and cook for approx. 1/2 hour. Remove from casserole dish and arrange on serving platter.

Sprinkle a little flour over the remaining pan drippings, add a little water and bring to a boil.

Remove from heat and add ice-cold flakes of butter to gravy, stirring with wire whisk. Strain gravy and pour over "Laubfröschle" ("tree-frog" or "greenback").

For a vegetarian version of this dish substitute the "Bratwurstbrät" with sautéed mushrooms or some type of grain, for example green kern (dried green wheat) or barley.

Wenn m'r erscht amol richtig gessa ond tronka hat – g'schafft isch glei

(After a hearty meal, a job is easily tackled)

Kratzete
Pancake Scratch

This pastry consists of a thick pancake, which can be served not only with a sweet or salty accompaniment, but also with fruit or vegetables.

Prepare batter by combining 4 egg yolks, 1¼ cups milk, 1 cup + ½ tablespoon flour, 1 dash salt and 2 tablespoons melted butter. Beat until smooth and let rest for 10 minutes.

Beat 4 egg whites until stiff and gently fold into egg yolk-mixture.

Melt fat in a large casserole, pour in batter and fry until golden in color. Turn with pancake turner and fry same as other side, adding extra fat if necessary.

Using two forks scratch ("zerkratzen," therefore the name of this dish) the pancake into pieces, turning frequently to fry on all sides.

Remove from casserole and serve with asparagus, spinach, special vegetables or salad.

If you care to serve "Kratzete" with cooked or stewed fruit, sprinkle with powdered sugar.

Wenn d'Küche nemme raucht, wird d'Liebe bald kalt

(Once the kitchen ceases to steam-up, love can also no longer be found)

Schlachtplatte
Butcher's Platter

During fall, "auf den Fildern bei Stuttgart" (in the Filder-region near Stuttgart) one can spot trucks with towering loads of "Spitzkraut" (sauerkraut), which nowhere else can be seen. This "Spitzkraut" is ideal for "Einmachen" (canning) as sauerkraut. Years ago, the "Kraut-Fäßle" (sauerkraut-barrel) provided kraut well into springtime (by the time the weather turned warm and the smell became very strong, the kraut had to be used up). However, due to present-day modern canning processing, sauerkraut is available the whole year through. If "Schlachtplatte" is listed on a Swabian menu you can be certain that garnished sauerkraut will be served. You may expect one liver sausage, one "Griebenwurst" (blood sausage), one slice pork flank and one slice beef. The last two accompaniments are cooked along with the sauerkraut, the sausages, however, are heated in the sauerkraut.

Sauté 1 large minced onion in 3 tablespoons lard until transparent in color. Loosen (by tearing apart) 35 ounces sauerkraut and sauté in onion mixture shortly. Then add enough water to just cover sauerkraut.

Peel and grate a large potato and add. Prepare an apple in the same manner and add also. Season with 10 juniper berries and 1 dash caraway and 1 bouillon cube.

Simmer over low heat for 45 minutes. Add additional water or white wine and 13½ ounces pork flank and the same amount lean beef (roast quality).

Cover and cook for ¾ hour longer.

One may also add pig's feet, pig's knuckles and paws (and also a tail), to enhance the flavor of the sauerkraut.

Once done, either heat liver and blood sausage in the sauerkraut or simmer in hot water, being careful not to boil, since the skins may burst. If desired season sauerkraut once more, spoon into a deep bowl and garnish with sausages. Serve with Spätzle or mashed potatoes. Authentic Swabian families insist on also serving split peas along with this dish. All that is left to say is “Prost Mahlzeit!”

Glossary

amol = einmal (once)
arg = sehr (very)
Args = Arges, Schlimmes (a terrible/dreadful happening)
auf d' Füß' kommen = auf die Füße kommen, gesund werden (to recover from sickness)
aufpfitzen = aufgehen (to rise, as for soufflé)
au G'sonde guet = auch Gesunden gut (healthy individuals also find it tasty)
aushausig, aushäusig = verschwenderisch; nur von gelegentlicher Großzügigkeit bestimmt (extravagant, lavish; can only be afforded once in a while)
Aushausigkeit = siehe aushausig (see aushausig)
drhoim = daheim, zu Hause (at home)
ebbes = etwas (something)
glei = gleich (right away)
Gsälz = Konfitüre (preserves, jam)
Guats = Gutes (something tasty)
Güetle = von Gut, kleines Garten-/Grundstück (small garden / piece of property used as a garden).

Gutsle = Weihnachtsgebäck von bestimmten Ausstecherformen (Christmas cookies of a special cut-out variety)
hebt, heben = vorhalten, anhalten, reichen, fassen, ergreifen, packen, festhalten (to accuse, to hinder, to hand over, to grasp, to seize, to grab, to hold on to)
Kender = Kinder (children)
knitz = schlau (clever)
Lensa = Linsen (lentils)
meh' = mehr (more)
mehlieren = in Mehl wenden (drench in flour)
m'r = man (one, as in one may eat more)
nacket = nackt (naked)
nemme = nicht mehr (no longer, no more)
no = dann (then)
nonder = hinunter (down)
nonderhänge = hinunterhängen (hang over, e.g., hang over edge of plate, refer to page 46)
Pärle = Pärchen (pair)
rädeln = in Scheiben schneiden (to slice)
Rädle = Scheiben, Scheibchen (slices)
räß = herb, rauh (pertaining to wine: new, slightly sour)

rezent = kräftig gewürzt (well-seasoned)

Saita = Saitenwürstchen, Brühwürstchen im Saitling (Schafsdarm) (special Swabian sausages or frankfurters)

's battet = es reicht, es genügt, es haut hin (that is enough, that will do)

Schnitz = kleines oder auch größeres Stück, z. B. von Kartoffeln oder Obst (small or even larger piece of e.g. potato or fruit)

scho = schon (already)

simmern = sanft unter dem Kochpunkt, pochieren; die Flüssigkeit kocht nicht wallend oder sprudelnd; die Oberfläche bewegt sich nur leicht (to simmer)

Spätzles-Schwob = Spätzlesmaschine; der Teig wird mit kräftigem Druck durch die Löcher eines im Handel erhältlichen Geräts gepreßt (special "Spätzle" noodle press; noodle dough is pressed with much effort through the holes of this special machine, which can be purchased in any Swabian household goods store)

Stich = Mengenangabe, etwa halber Eßlöffel (measured amount, approx. 1/2 tablespoon)

Trenka = trinken (to drink, drinking)

Überzwerch = Querrippe unterhalb des Rinderrückens (crossrib below back of beef)
verheben = sich zurückhalten, siehe “wer’s Dickwerden ...” (to control oneself, refer to “those who cannot watch calories . . ., page 113).
verkleppern = verquirlen, von klappern, das klappernde Geräusch, das beim Verquirlen entsteht (to beat with fork or whisk, clicking noise resulting from beating motion)
Veschper = das Vesper; kalte Mahlzeit anstelle des Nachmittagskaffees oder frühes Abendessen (early meal instead of the late afternoon coffeetime or an early dinner)
Wengert = Weinberg (vineyard)
Wer’s Dickwerden nicht verheben kann = wem’s so gut schmeckt, daß ihm eine mögliche Gewichtszunahme gleichgültig ist (those who cannot “hold back” putting on weight = those who enjoy the meal so much, that they are not concerned with calories or possibly gaining weight)

General Index (English)

General Index (German)